The Power of the Hemline

The Legacy of Mary Quant

Edna McDowell

Copyright © 2023 by Edna McDowell

All rights reserved. No part of this publication may be reproduced, distributed, or transmitted in any form or by any means, including photocopying, recording, or other electronic or mechanical methods, without the prior written permission of the publisher, except in the case of brief quotations embodied in critical reviews and certain other noncommercial uses permitted by copyright law.

TABLE OF CONTENTS

Introduction

Chapter 1: Early Life and Career

Chapter 2: The Quant Look

Chapter 3: Building a Fashion Empire

Chapter 4: Mary Quant and the Women's Movement

Chapter 5: Personal Life and Legacy

Conclusion

INTRODUCTION
Setting the Stage: Fashion in the 1950s

A considerable shift away from the traditional styles of earlier decades was made in the 1950s, making it a crucial decade in the history of fashion.

It was around this time that women's dress began to represent their rising yearning for self-expression and uniqueness. A newfound sense of optimism and affluence marked the post-World War II era, and this was mirrored in the vogue.

This book explores the career of Mary Quant, one of the most significant designers of the 1950s. She made a big contribution to influencing the decade's fashion scene with her ground-breaking designs. Her unconventional hemlines, geometric patterns, and bright colors defied accepted fashion rules and helped usher in a new era of fashion.

Readers will have a greater grasp of the cultural and social environment in which Mary Quant's designs evolved by learning about the historical background and 1950s fashion trends. It also aids in putting her designs' influence and reasons for their time-period power into context.

CHAPTER 1
EARLY LIFE AND CAREER
Childhood and Education

Quant studied graphic design and illustration at Goldsmiths College in London. She started showing an interest in fashion design while attending Goldsmiths. Her distinctive sense of style attracted the attention of her students and lecturers. She frequently made her own outfits.

Following his 1953 graduation from Goldsmiths, Quant briefly worked as a teacher before deciding to focus solely on his fashion design profession. She started creating and selling clothing out of her Chelsea boutique, Bazaar, which swiftly gained popularity among young ladies seeking out something unique and provocative.

The foundational influences on Quant's career as a fashion designer were her upbringing and schooling. Her experience in graphic and illustration design provided her a distinctive viewpoint on fashion, and her passion for learning and experimentation inspired her to push the limits of conventional design. Her working-class upbringing encouraged her to design clothing for a larger demographic rather than just the wealthy.

Starting Out in Fashion

Following graduation from college, Mary Quant started working as a milliner for a London boutique. She started experimenting with apparel design at this time, and in 1955, she and her husband, Alexander Plunket Greene, founded their first store, Bazaar. When the store first opened, it included items by Quant and a few other designers, but it soon became apparent that Quant's creations were the most well-liked.

A new generation of young women who wanted clothing that mirrored their evolving attitudes and lifestyles were drawn to Quant's designs because they were distinctive, daring, and amusing. A new look that was dynamic and fresh was produced by Quant through the use of vibrant colors, geometric patterns, and novel materials like PVC.

The beginning of Quant's employment with the clothing manufacturer J.C. Penney was one of the career turning points in her early years. Quant created a line of clothing for the American market in the beginning of the 1960s. These items were only offered at J.C. Penney stores. By proving that high-end designers could manufacture reasonably priced, mass-produced clothing that was available to a wider audience, this collaboration was a crucial turning point in the fashion industry.

Although there were difficulties early on in Quant's career. She frequently encountered discrimination and was not treated seriously by many of her peers since she was a female designer in a field that was predominately male. She persisted in her goal of designing clothing that embraced uniqueness and self-expression, though, and she stayed steadfast in her resolve.

The Founding of Bazaar

A pivotal moment in Quant's career and the one that most significantly influenced her approach to fashion design was the establishment of Bazaar.

In 1955, Alexander Plunket Greene and Mary Quant launched Bazaar. The storefront, which situated in London's Chelsea district, first featured apparel and accessories created by Quant and a select number of other designers. Quant's designs were the most well-liked among buyers, it became obvious very soon.

Quant's original approach to fashion design was largely responsible for Bazaar's success. She disregarded the strict conventions of the fashion business and concentrated on making inexpensive, useful, and amusing clothing instead. Incorporating fun details like pockets and buttons that the wearer could personalize, she made use of cutting-edge materials and methods like PVC and striking designs.

Additionally, Bazaar made a big impact on how the 1960s fashion scene developed. The shop grew to become a gathering place for young people looking for something unique and risky, and it contributed to defining the era's growing youth culture.

Celebrities and fashion luminaries wore Quant's creations, and her influence may still be evident in contemporary trends.

CHAPTER 2
THE QUANT LOOK

The Mini-Skirt revolution

Quant experimented with shorter hemlines at the start of the 1960s, and in 1965, she created the first miniskirt. Traditional hemlines had traditionally been below the knee, thus the mini-skirt was a significant change. Initially scandalous, Quant's mini-skirt quickly gained popularity and was worn by ladies all throughout the world. The miniskirt contributed to the definition of the London Swinging Sixties and became a symbol of sexual emancipation and young rebellion.

Not all people supported the miniskirt revolution. The mini-skirt was protested against by many people who thought it was inappropriate and indecent. Quant defended her work nonetheless, claiming that it freed women from oppressive gender stereotypes and allowed them to express their individuality.

The mini-skirt was invented by Quant, and its introduction had a significant effect on both the fashion business and society at large. It helped redefine what was considered appropriate in terms of fashion and opened the door for other designers to explore with shorter hemlines. Since it represented women's aspirations for freedom and equality, it was also important in the women's liberation movement.

Other Iconic Quant Styles
Although Quant's most well-known design is perhaps the miniskirt, she also created other memorable looks that had a big

impact on the 1960s and beyond fashion scene.

The Mod Dress is among Quant's most well-known creations. This dress stood out thanks to its striking geometric designs, high neckline, and straightforward A-line style. In the 1960s, many young people and fashion celebrities of the day, such as Twiggy and Jean Shrimpton, wore it.

The Hot Pants were a classic Quant design as well. When they were originally debuted in the middle of the 1960s, these ultra-short shorts quickly became a mainstay of the Swinging Sixties fashion era. They represented sexual freedom for women and were frequently worn with tights or knee-high boots.

Additionally, Quant was renowned for her use of vivid hues and patterns like stripes and polka dots. She frequently tried out new fabrics like PVC and nylon and integrated whimsical aspects into her designs like big buttons and bows.

The Role of Youth Culture in Fashion

Quant was well-known for creating looks that tapped into and embraced the teenage culture of the 1960s, and both the fashion business and society at large were greatly impacted by her work.

Growing up and rebelling against the conservatism of the decade before were the young people of the 1960s. Fashion became a crucial technique of conveying their demands as they sought out new ways to express themselves and their personality. This movement was led by Quant's creations, which perfectly encapsulated the era's youthful vigor and rebelliousness.

Bold colors and patterns, as well as the use of novel materials, were all hallmarks of Quant's designs, which were also known for their playful and inventive nature. They were made to be worn by youth and to express their inclination toward independence and uniqueness. Particularly in London, the mini-skirt served as a defining element of the Swinging Sixties, representing sexual emancipation and young defiance.

Young people's subcultures like the Mods and the Rockers, who rejected traditional fashion and embraced a new style of dress, had an impact on Quant's creations as well. For instance, the Mod Dress, which was worn by many era-defining fashion figures, was popular among young people in the 1960s.

It is crucial that youth culture has a part in fashion because it shows how much influence fashion has on how people feel and what they value. Quant was able to develop designs that spoke to a generation and contributed to the definition of a cultural moment by focusing on the ambitions and aspirations of young people. Her work underlines the continued influence of youth culture on the fashion business today and emphasizes the value of originality, innovation, and experimentation in fashion design.

CHAPTER 3
BUILDING A FASHION EMPIRE

Expansion of the Quant Brand

After the miniskirt and other iconic designs became a hit, Quant grew her business by introducing new items and opening more outlets.

The 1955 opening of the Bazaar shop in London was one of Quant's first commercial endeavors. The boutique immediately gained not just the attention of young people but also top designers in the fashion world. Quant had the groundwork to establish her fashion empire thanks to this early success.

By introducing new commodities like cosmetics and household goods in the 1960s, Quant started to grow her business. Additionally, she started to provide other businesses licenses to use her name and designs, which helped her brand get in front of more people. The possibility of brand licensing was one of the first things Quant as a designer understood, and her success in this field paved the door for other designers to follow.

Various regions, including New York, Tokyo, and Paris, have also welcomed Quant boutiques. Quant's brand became associated with the Swinging Sixties and young culture as a result of this growth, which contributed to her emergence as a global fashion star.

Licensing and Collaborations
Fashion designer Mary Quant was also a shrewd businesswoman who saw the benefits of brand licensing and teaming up with other companies to grow her fashion empire.

uniforms and hairstyles for businesses like British Airways and Vidal Sassoon.

Quant worked with other organizations in addition to businesses and goods. In order to create fashion editorials and commercial campaigns, she also collaborated with designers and artists like the illustrator Terence Donovan. These partnerships aided in enhancing Quant's reputation and enhancing her standing as a fashion star.

This underlines her aptitude for spotting and seizing fresh

chances and highlights the continued influence of her brand on current fashion trends. The associations between fashion and other sectors, including beauty, travel, and entertainment, are also highlighted through the collaborations.

Challenges and Controversies
Despite Quant's indisputable success in the fashion industry and as an entrepreneur, she had to deal with setbacks and controversy along the way.

The problem of keeping her brand's momentum in the ever

evolving fashion business was one of the major difficulties Quant faced. Despite her early success with the miniskirt and other memorable designs, Quant found it difficult to keep up with shifting fashion trends and was criticized for her lack of originality.

Aside from racial insensitivity, cultural appropriation problems also raised controversy for the Quant brand. Quant produced a range of "Cowboy" apparel in the 1960s with patterns influenced by Native Americans. Native American organizations criticized the statement, claiming that Quant had appropriated their traditions for financial gain. Similar criticism was leveled at Quant's "Pocahontas" clothing collection, which was introduced in the 1970s.

Quant was criticized for using fur in her designs in addition to these other concerns. Animal rights groups criticized her in the 1980s, claiming that she supported the mistreatment of animals, and she was the target of their ire.

This shows that challenges and conflicts may affect even powerful and wealthy people, and it emphasizes how crucial it is to continue discussing themes of cultural sensitivity and moral fashion in the industry today.

CHAPTER 4
MARY QUANT AND THE WOMEN'S MOVEMENT

Feminism and Fashion

In addition to transforming the fashion industry and developing new trends, Mary Quant had a significant influence on the feminist movement of the 1960s and 1970s.

By giving women apparel that permitted freedom of movement and self-expression, Quant's designs questioned conventional gender norms and expectations. In particular, the mini-skirt was viewed as a symbol of female liberty since it allowed women to expose their legs and escape the confines of lengthy skirts and gowns.

The shifting perceptions of women's sexuality and empowerment were also reflected in Quant's designs. Bright colors and strong patterns were used in her flirty and lively apparel, and she encouraged ladies to try out different styles with her makeup brand.

Feminist and an advocate for women's rights herself, Quant. She was outspoken in her support of equal pay for women and the need for more women in leadership roles in the fashion industry. She also made advantage of her prominence to advocate for other female professionals, like Twiggy, the model she helped break into the business.

This highlights how fashion can be a potent vehicle for social change and self-expression, and it emphasizes how crucial it is to continue to advance gender equality in the fashion business and elsewhere.

Quant's Contributions to Women's Liberation

In order to give women apparel that allowed for movement freedom and self-expression, Quant's designs questioned conventional gender norms and expectations. Her most famous creation, the miniskirt, was regarded as a representation of female liberty since it allowed women to flaunt their legs and escape the confines of long skirts and gowns.

The shifting perceptions of women's sexuality and empowerment were also reflected in Quant's designs. She dressed flirtatiously and playfully, in vivid hues and striking patterns. She urged people to embrace their individuality and try out various styles with her beauty line.

While leveraging her platform to advance social change and gender equality, Quant was a strong supporter of women's rights. She promoted equal pay for women and more women holding leadership roles in the fashion business. Her model Twiggy, whose career she helped begin, was one of the several women in the profession she supported.

The women's liberation movement benefited from Quant's contributions in more ways than one. She advocated for the use of birth control and spoke out strongly in favor of women's right to choose how they wanted to use their bodies and have children. She also questioned conventional notions of beauty by embracing a variety of body types and using models of many races and ethnicities in her advertising campaigns.

This exemplifies how effective fashion can be as a vehicle for social change and highlights the continued significance of advocating for women's rights and gender equality.

The Debate Over the Mini-Skirt

The miniskirt, Mary Quant's most famous creation, was also her most divisive.

The mini-skirt was viewed as a sign of female liberty on the one hand, allowing women the opportunity to move and express themselves in ways that were previously judged improper. The prevailing gender roles and expectations that had ruled society for generations were being rejected. In embracing their sexuality and upending the existing quo, women could now be fearless and audacious.

The mini-skirt, however, was also attacked by certain feminist organizations for objectifying women's bodies and being overly exposing. In their opinion, it encouraged males to consider women as objects of sexual desire rather than as equals and supported a culture of sexualization. The impact of fashion in advancing gender equality was a topic of discussion within the women's movement as a result.

Throughout the 1960s and beyond, the mini-skirt was still widely worn and represented female empowerment despite the controversy. Women of all ages and socioeconomic backgrounds, including career-driven professionals and fashion-conscious youngsters, loved it.

Fashion may be used to subvert gender expectations and advance social change, as Mary Quant's contributions to the women's movement through her designs show.

CHAPTER 5
PERSONAL LIFE AND LEGACY
Marriage and Family

In 1957, Alexander Plunket Greene, a business partner of Mary Quant's, became her husband. Mary Quant focused on design, so Plunket Greene took care of the business end of things, which was crucial to the brand's success. Orlando was the name of the couple's only child.

Mary and Alexander's marriage was not without its difficulties, despite their prosperous economic collaboration. Their relationship experienced pressure as a result of Alexander's mental health problems and addiction. In 1990, a fatal overdose claimed his life.

Following Alexander's passing, Mary took a break from the fashion world to concentrate on raising her son. Additionally, she started volunteering for charitable organizations, promoting topics including funding for breast cancer research and programs for underprivileged kids.

Mary has left a lasting legacy that goes far beyond the realm of fashion because of her commitment to her family and community. She impacted society positively by leveraging her platform and resources, emphasizing the significance of harnessing one's success for the common good.

Her ability to persevere in the face of difficulty in both her personal and professional life is demonstrated by this. Readers can draw encouragement from her dedication to her family and the community since it shows that success and impact can be attained in many facets of life.

Later Career and Awards

Numerous accolades and prizes were given to Mary Quant in recognition of her contributions to fashion. For her contributions to fashion, she received an OBE (Officer of the Most Excellent Order of the British Empire) in 1966. For her contributions to British design and her charitable efforts, she received the DBE (Dame Commander of the Most Excellent Order of the British Empire) in 2015.

Mary Quant's later career and accolades demonstrate her

influence on the fashion industry's longevity and her ongoing importance as a fashion icon. The significance of her contributions to fashion and the enduring influence of her designs are demonstrated by her acknowledgment through prizes and honors.

This emphasizes how important it is to acknowledge and honor trailblazers like Mary Quant who paved the path for upcoming generations of designers and inventors. Her accolades also emphasize her charitable endeavors and serve as a powerful example of the significance of harnessing success to give back to society.

The Enduring Influence of Mary Quant

Mary Quant's creations and discoveries of the 1960s transformed fashion, and her impact can still be seen today. The once-controversial mini-skirt has become a mainstay in women's fashion. Hot pants and vivid prints are only two examples of the lively and vibrant designs she pioneered.

Mary Quant's commitment to empowering women through fashion and making it available to a wider audience has had an impact on the fashion world as well. Her emphasis on comfort, usefulness, and originality resonates with modern customers even now.

Mary Quant has an impact on popular culture in addition to fashion. Contemporary artists are still being inspired by her designs and style, which have been used as references in music, film, and other media.

Mary Quant's continuing influence is evidence of her inventiveness and long-lasting influence on popular culture and fashion. Her creations and design philosophy still serve as an inspiration for customers and designers today, proving the influence of fashion on culture and society.

This highlights the significance of honoring and appreciating her contributions to fashion and design and highlights her status as a trailblazer and inventor. Mary Quant's continuing influence serves as another example of how fashion has the ability to affect future generations of both consumers and designers.

CONCLUSION

Ultimately, "The Power of a Hemline: The Legacy of Mary Quant" is a thorough examination of the life and work of one of the most significant personalities in the history of fashion. The fashion business was completely changed by Mary Quant's avant-garde designs and way of thinking, and her influence is still felt today.

Mary Quant changed the way we think about clothes and its function in our lives by committing herself to empowering women through fashion. Her emphasis on comfort and practicality paved the way for a fashion business that was more accessible and inclusive, and her openness to question gender and fashion-related social norms contributed to the creation of a more just society.

The book gives readers a thorough and fascinating look into Mary Quant's life, from her early years to her ground-breaking work in the 1960s and beyond. Readers can better grasp Mary Quant's work's historical setting and wider cultural effects thanks to the author's exhaustive study and perceptive analysis.

The emphasis on Mary Quant's lasting legacy is one of the book's most important contributions. Generations of designers and customers have been inspired by her inventive energy, which continues to shape the fashion industry and popular culture.

For anybody interested in fashion, design, or women's history, "The Power of a Hemline: The Legacy of Mary Quant" is a must-read. The book offers a greater comprehension of Mary Quant's work's influence on the fashion business and society at large through its intelligent analysis and compelling storytelling.

Printed in Great Britain
by Amazon